To:

....

From:

....

Date:

....

ZONDERVAN

The Weekly Faith Project

Copyright © 2019 by Zondervan

Requests for information should be addressed to: Zondervan,
3900 Sparks Dr., SE, Grand Rapids, MI 49546

ISBN 978-0-310-45332-1

Cover design and hand-lettering: Connie Gabbert
Cover illustration: Tiffany Lausen
Interior design: Lori Lynch

Printed in China

19 20 21 22 23 / GRI / 16 15 14 13 12 11 10 9 8 7 6 5 4 3 2 1

THE WEEKLY
Faith
Project

*A Challenge to Journal, Reflect, and
Cultivate a Genuine Faith*

ZONDERVAN®

Contents

Faith Is . . .

What Faith Does

When Faith Is Hard

Faith Is for Growing

Faith Is Rewarded . . .

How to Use This Journal

For it is by grace you have been saved, through faith.

Ephesians 2:8

Faith is a living thing, growing and flourishing as you bask in the light of God's promises and drink in the evidences of His faithfulness. But faith starves when left alone in the cold and dark of busyness, neglect, and doubt.

This book is intended to help you nourish your faith, to help it thrive and grow. Each week you'll find thoughts, questions, and Scriptures for you to ponder. Doubts and fears will be carefully pruned away as you are encouraged to sink your roots deep into the truths of God's promises, the steadfastness of His love, and the reality of His faithfulness.

Record your thoughts, your prayers, and your questions here. Take note of all the ways you see God working in your life. And watch as your faith grows stronger, deeper, richer—blooming bright and beautiful as you draw ever nearer to God.

Faith Is...

Faith is believing God is who He says He is and that He will do all He says He will do.

Faith Is . . . Believing

*Faith shows the reality of what we hope for; it
is the evidence of things we cannot see.*

Hebrews 11:1 NLT

Faith is believing. But it's more than that too. It's trusting that every word from God is true. Because every one is. It's expecting God to keep every promise He makes. Because He will. It's accepting that His love for you is perfectly complete and unconditional. Because it is. Faith isn't simply believing; it's allowing that faith to define who you are and who you will become.

How do you define faith? How does your faith define you?

Faith to me is knowing what will be will be. That there is already a plan and I must believe it is for the best. I live each day to the best of my abilities w/ faith in HIS plan.

I want to learn to grow in His word. Understand it and apply it my my life everyday. I want to trust the word, despite it be an edited version from man. I want to have faith that scripture is what He wants to be translated to My life and that there is a reason for revealing those particular words to me @ the time they are brought into the light.
FAITH & Application♡

Faith Is . . . Knowing the Character of God

God is light; in him there is no darkness at all.

1 John 1:5

Faith knows—and trusts—who God is. And who is He? He is the One who never leaves—not as God the Father (Deuteronomy 31:6), not as God the Son (Matthew 28:20), and not as God the Holy Spirit (John 14:16). He never lies (Titus 1:2), He never does wrong (Deuteronomy 32:3–4), and He never fails to keep a promise (Numbers 23:19). And you can put your full faith in Him because neither He nor His Word *ever* changes (Hebrews 13:8, Matthew 24:35).

In a world where everything changes, how crucial is it for you to know that God never does?

Change is scary. Especially lately. I feel like everything is changing. My thoughts, my actions, my life decisions, parenting, work and even friends. Despite, it feels RIGHT. I finally feel like I'm on a path that has been waiting for me all along. I know that He has been waiting patiently for me, loving me despite my detours. HE has been my constant. Unconditional Love. ♡

And it makes my heart happy knowing HE is smiling from above. Proud that I am finally figuring it out.

WEEK 3
Faith Is . . . Knowing Who You Are

"Do not fear, for I have redeemed you; I have summoned you by name; you are mine."

Isaiah 43:1

Faith is allowing God to define who you are. Not the world. Not family, friend, or enemy. And who does God say you are? You are His own treasured possession (1 Peter 2:9), His lavishly loved child (1 John 3:1). He knows every hair on your head and every tear you cry (Luke 12:7, Psalm 56:8). He writes your name on the palm of His hand (Isaiah 49:16). God knows you, and He calls you "Mine."

Take a few moments to read the verses listed above for yourself. What do these verses say to your heart about who you really are?

....

....

....

....

Why is it so important—to you and your faith—to allow God to define who you are, rather than the world or anyone in it?

....

....

....

....

....

....

....

....

....

....

....

....

Faith Is . . . Necessary

>>>>>><<<<<<

*Without faith it is impossible to please God, because
anyone who comes to him must believe that he exists
and that he rewards those who earnestly seek him.*

Hebrews 11:6

F aith is necessary. For salvation, yes. For heaven, yes. But
also for this: *pleasing God.* Just as the child longs to please
the father, the faithful heart longs to please the heavenly
Father. Yes, there are things you do that make Him smile, that
make Him sing (Zephaniah 3:17). But if your desire is to truly
please Him, give Him your trust and your faith.

What do you believe pleases God? Is faith your first
answer? Or do you get caught up more in the doing
than the believing?

....

....

....

....

Why do you believe your faith pleases God? Consider John 3:16 and 2 Peter 3:9. What do these verses tell you about what God most wants?

WEEK 5
Faith Is . . . Relying on God

When you ask, you must believe and not doubt,
because the one who doubts is like a wave of the sea,
blown and tossed by the wind. That person should
not expect to receive anything from the Lord. Such a
person is double-minded and unstable in all they do.

James 1:6–8

Believe and not doubt. Those words are sobering, convicting, even a bit frightening. Because it's so easy to doubt, isn't it? The key lies in verse 8: the person who doubts is double-minded. That doesn't mean that you never have any doubts about how or when God will answer; it is that you never doubt that God *is* the answer.

Are you double-minded—relying on the world and on your own resources to see you through—even as you turn to God in prayer? Or are you fully relying on Him to give you the answers you need?

....

....

When you pray, are you sure God's answers will always be what is best for you? Consider Jeremiah 29:11 and Romans 8:28. What do these promises tell you about God's answers to your prayers? Do they strengthen your faith?

....

....

....

....

....

....

....

....

....

....

....

WEEK 6
Faith Is . . . Forgiven

Oh, what joy for those whose disobedience is
forgiven, whose sins are put out of sight.

Romans 4:7 NLT

There is no need to carry all that baggage around. The mistakes you've made—and the ones you're going to make. The bad choices. The thoughtless words. The moments of outright rebellion. When you have faith, you can take all those things and leave them at the foot of the cross, knowing the price for those sins has already been paid. Faith means freedom from the penalties of sin—and it means you are forgiven.

When you lay your sins before God, what does He do with them? Consider 1 John 1:9 and Psalm 103:12.

....

....

....

....

....

Be honest. What do you expect of yourself? In your home, family, friendships, and, yes, faith? What does God expect of you in each of those areas? Begin your answer by reading Micah 6:8—and notice that the word "perfect" is nowhere in it.

WEEK 7
Faith Is . . . Accepting Grace

>>>>>>———<<<<<<

God raised us up with Christ and seated us with him in the heavenly realms in Christ Jesus, in order that in the coming ages he might show the incomparable riches of his grace, expressed in his kindness to us in Christ Jesus.

Ephesians 2:6–7

Faith doesn't only mean you are forgiven. It doesn't only mean that you are freed from the penalty your sins earned. Faith means you are given grace—all the richest blessings of heaven that you could never, ever earn.

Forgiveness is sweet relief; grace is unending joy and delight.

How would you define the difference between *forgiveness* and *grace*?

....

....

....

....

....

....

....

....

....

....

....

....

....

....

....

....

WEEK 8
Faith Is . . . Healing

>>>>>>><<<<<<

"If I only touch his cloak, I will be healed."

Matthew 9:21

Twelve years. That's how long she had bled, how long she had been ostracized, how long she had suffered at the hands of doctors who took her money and left her . . . still bleeding. But then Jesus came, and she dared to believe. *"If I only . . ."* You know the rest of this story from Matthew 9. She touched His cloak, and He said to her, "Daughter . . . your faith has healed you" (v. 22). Because faith is healing.

Faith reaches out to the One who heals and makes you whole. What is there in your life—heart, mind, body, or soul—that needs to be healed and made whole?

....

....

....

....

....

While healing is sometimes everything we hope and expect, sometimes it is not. What is the greatest healing Jesus offers? Consider 1 Peter 2:24 as you answer.

....

....

....

....

....

....

....

....

....

....

....

....

Faith Is . . . Knowing God Is Able

God is able to do whatever he promises.

Romans 4:21 NLT

Faith means knowing God is able to do all that He has promised. You may not understand how. You may not know where or when. It may seem utterly, completely impossible. But for all the things you do not know—for all the odds stacked against you—in faith, there is one thing you *do* know: God is able, and He will deliver that which He has promised to you.

Begin a list of all that God has promised you—and add to it with each new promise you discover in His Word. Begin with Psalm 121.

Which of God's promises is most important to you and your faith right now? Write out a prayer of praise declaring that you know He is able to keep that promise in your life.

....

....

....

....

....

....

....

....

....

....

....

....

....

WEEK 10
Faith Is . . . Love

>>>>>><<<<<<

The only thing that counts is faith
expressing itself through love.
Galatians 5:6

God is love . . . and so faith in God must have love. It's loving God with all your heart and soul and mind and strength (Mark 12:30). And it is accepting that God's love for you is both endless and unconditional (Romans 8:38–39). Because God's love for you gives you every reason to have faith, and your faith gives you every reason to show the world how much you love Him.

Why does God's love for you give you every reason to put your faith in Him?

....

....

....

....

....

Does your faith express itself in love? Read 1 Corinthians 13:1–3. Why do you believe the expression of love is so important to faith—your own and others'?

....

....

....

....

....

....

....

....

....

....

....

Faith Is . . . Taking God at His Word

*For I myself am a man under authority, with
soldiers under me. I tell this one, "Go," and he
goes; and that one, "Come," and he comes. I say
to my servant, "Do this," and he does it.*

Luke 7:8

S ay the word, and my servant will be healed" (Luke 7:7). Such was the faith of a humble Roman centurion, and his faith amazed even Jesus (v. 9). That man knew—what all those who put their faith in God know—that He is able to do all He has said He will do. So when God says He will forgive and save, help and guide, love and protect . . . faith takes God at His word.

Compare the faith of this centurion to the faith of Thomas in John 20:24–29. Which one more resembles you and your faith?

....

....

....

Is there any area of your faith where you most struggle to take God at His word? Write out a prayer asking God to show you His faithfulness.

....

....

....

....

....

....

....

....

....

....

....

....

WEEK 12
Faith Is . . . Knowing God Is Faithful

For the word of the LORD is right and
true; he is faithful in all he does.

Psalm 33:4

Just as you are able to love God because He first loved you, you can be faithful because God was—and is and always will be—faithful to you. What does that mean? It means God's actions toward you are always loving and good, and He is always working in your life to do what is just right for you (Psalm 25:10, Romans 8:28).

How long is God faithful? How far will His faithfulness reach? Discover the answers in Psalm 117:2 and Psalm 36:5. What does this kind of faithfulness mean to you?

God's faithfulness—His love and mercy and compassion—
are as certain as the sunrise (Lamentations 3:22–23).
This week, seek out the sunrise. How is it a reflection of
His faithfulness to you?

WEEK 13
Faith Is . . . Choosing

>>>>>>>───><───<<<<<<

As for me and my family, we will serve the LORD.
Joshua 24:15 NCV

Faith is choosing to believe . . . *and to keep on believing.* It's not a once-and-done choice. Rather, it is a decision made many, many times each day. Sometimes consciously, sometimes instinctively. Because each and every day, you will be confronted with the temptations, the traps and snares the evil one tosses down before you, like so many gauntlets challenging your faith. Faith is looking the devil in the eye and saying, "As for me, I will serve the Lord."

Is faith an easy choice for you? What makes it more difficult at times? Easier at times?

....

....

....

....

....

Psalm 119:30 is about choosing the "way of faithfulness." What is that way? And does your life show the world you have chosen "the way of faithfulness"?

....

....

....

....

....

....

....

....

....

....

....

....

What Faith Does

Faith is living out all you believe.

Faith Dares

>>>>>>>——<<<<<<

*Now to him who is able to do immeasurably more
than all we ask or imagine, according to his
power that is at work within us, to him be glory
in the church and in Christ Jesus throughout
all generations, for ever and ever! Amen.*

Ephesians 3:20–21

Faith has nothing to do with settling. It is daring and confident. God has given you a gift, a passion that He wants you to use—whether it's big and bold and out in the world or gentle and quiet and behind the scenes. So don't settle for going through the motions. Ask God, and then watch as He enables you to do more than you could ever imagine!

Have you discovered your passion, your gift for giving back to the One who has given you so much? Make a list of the things you do that bring you joy, and then make a list of the needs around you. Does your passion lie where the two lists meet?

....

....

....

Let your faith be bold. Write out a prayer asking God to open your eyes to all the ways He imagines you serving Him.

....

....

....

....

....

....

....

....

....

....

....

WEEK 15
Faith Reflects God

>>>>>><<<<<<

*"The LORD, the LORD, the compassionate and
gracious God, slow to anger, abounding in love
and faithfulness, maintaining love to thousands,
and forgiving wickedness, rebellion and sin."*

Exodus 34:6–7

The Lord abounds in faithfulness to His people. What does that faithfulness look like in a life? It's the compassion that moved the heart of Jesus to help and to heal. It's His gracious kindness that fed a hungry crowd and called a desperate woman *daughter*. Faithfulness is patient, and it is love without limits. If you want to know what the faithfulness of God looks like—it looks like Jesus (John 14:9). And your faithfulness should lead you to look like Him.

Does your life reflect the faithfulness of God? Is it compassionate, kind, patient, and loving? What can you do to make your life a clearer reflection of Him?

....

....

....

Look for opportunities this week to reflect the faithfulness of God with your words and actions. Make a note of those opportunities—and your response to them—here.

....

....

....

....

....

....

....

....

....

....

....

Faith Moves Mountains

"Truly I tell you, if you have faith as small as a mustard seed, you can say to this mountain, 'Move from here to there,' and it will move. Nothing will be impossible for you."

Matthew 17:20

A millimeter, the tip of pen, the sprinkle on a cupcake. That's the size of a mustard seed. Impossibly small. Yet Jesus declares even that tiny bit of faith is enough to move a mountain. Sometimes faith moves the mountain in an instant—the storm stills, the lame leap, and the broken are made whole again. Sometimes the mountain moves pebble by pebble, stone by stone—and faith must stretch for the marathon and not the sprint. One thing is certain, though: faith will move mountains.

Think of a time in your life—or in someone else's life—when the impossible suddenly became possible and the mountain moved right before your eyes. How did that impact your faith?

....

....

Think of a time when the mountain moved, but only one tiny pebble at a time. Is it harder to keep your faith in such times? When that last pebble finally yielded, what was the real reward—the moved mountain or the strengthening of your faith?

....

....

....

....

....

....

....

....

....

....

Faith Sees the Fingerprints

By faith we understand that the universe was
formed at God's command, so that what is seen
was not made out of what was visible.

Hebrews 11:3

Faith sees the wonders of creation and recognizes that creation all began with a word. *His* word. And once you realize that the God who set the planets in their places, who calls each and every star by its name, is the *same* God who left heaven to rescue you—well, that changes everything. Faith is transformed from being big and out there in the universe to being up close and in your heart. Faith rejoices because it looks at the world . . . and sees the fingerprints of God.

Just as a potter leaves fingerprints on the clay, God has left His fingerprints all over His creation. Where do you most see the fingerprints of God?

....

....

....

Read Psalm 19:1–4. What words do the heavens speak to you?

WEEK 18
Faith Trusts

>>>>>⟩⟩⟩≺⟨⟨⟨⟨⟨

"Don't let your hearts be troubled.
Trust in God, and trust in me."
John 14:1 NCV

D on't let your hearts be troubled." These are the words of the
One who endured every kind of trouble, every temptation,
every sorrow and pain—and yet remained faithful. In other
words, when Jesus tells you not to be troubled, He knows
what He's talking about. He faced all those troubles—and He
overcame. That alone makes Him worthy of your trust, worthy
of your faith. But there's more . . . because Jesus promises to
help you overcome your troubles too.

Jesus never promised that faith would free you from
troubles; rather, He promised to help you overcome them (John
16:33). Have you seen this truth in your own life?

As you think of the troubles you have faced with
Jesus by your side, how does His past faithfulness
help you face the troubles of today—and not worry
about the troubles of tomorrow?

....

....

Consider the promises of Isaiah 43:1–5. What do they tell you about troubles and facing them with God on your side?

....

....

....

....

....

....

....

....

....

....

....

....

WEEK 19
Faith Gives

>>>>>><<<<<<

As Jesus looked up, . . . He also saw a poor widow put in
two very small copper coins. "Truly I tell you," he said,
"this poor widow has put in more than all the others.
All these people gave their gifts out of their wealth; but
she out of her poverty put in all she had to live on."

Luke 21:1-4

"A poor widow." Those three little words tell you so much—her station in life, her poverty, her aloneness. It would have been so easy, so tempting to hold tight to those last two copper coins. Instead, she chose to let them go and to hold tight to her Lord. Because faith trusts God to provide all that is truly needed. And because it trusts, faith is not afraid to give.

Do you ever find yourself afraid to give? Do you hold back . . . just in case? Ask yourself these questions: What do you think happened to that widow after she left the temple? Do you believe she went hungry? Or do you believe God made a way to meet her needs?

. . . .

. . . .

Read the words of Luke 6:38. In them you'll find both a challenge and a promise. What does that challenge look like in your life? How have you seen God keep this promise?

Faith Loves . . . and Does

"Truly I tell you, whatever you did for one of the least of these brothers and sisters of mine, you did for me."

Matthew 25:40

Faith loves . . . and it does. And not from afar. It loves up close and in the trenches. Faith spoons out meals to the hungry and offers cool water on a hot summer's day. It welcomes the stranger and invites the lonely in. It visits prisons and hospitals. Faith doesn't worry about being seen; it simply sees to the needs. Because faith loves not only with the heart but with the hands and feet. Why? Because faith does what Jesus did.

There are people our world sees as "the least of these." But how do you believe Jesus sees these people? How does He want you to see them?

. . . .

. . . .

. . . .

Most every day, you'll encounter some of "the least of these." Do those encounters reflect your faith? What can you do to show these people the love of Jesus?

Faith Asks the Father

>>>>>✕<<<<<

*I will pray to the LORD, and he will answer
me from his holy mountain.*

Psalm 3:4 NCV

Faith asks the Father. It kneels down, lifting hands and heart—and knows He will answer (Isaiah 65:24). Not just with *any* answer but with *the* answer that's both perfect and just for you.

When you need something—big or small—ask your Father. Lay it before His throne, and look to Him for His answer. It will come, in the perfect way and the perfect time. And don't just ask Him for what you need to survive. Dare to ask Him for what you need to thrive.

When you pray, God bends down to listen (Psalm 116:2). What does this tell you about how God views your prayers? How does this encourage your faith?

Read Matthew 7:7–8, James 4:2, and Isaiah 65:24. What do these verses tell you about God's willingness to hear your faith-filled prayers, how He will answer them—and when He will answer?

....

....

46

Think about how you answer the needs of those you love. What do you try to bring to their lives? Now look at the promise offered in Matthew 7:9–11. What does this tell you about God's answers and what He hopes they will bring to your life?

....

....

....

....

....

....

....

....

....

....

....

Faith Seeks the Will of God

This is the confidence we have in approaching God: that if we ask anything according to his will, he hears us. And if we know that he hears us—whatever we ask—we know that we have what we asked of him.

1 John 5:14–15

First John offers not one, not two, but three powerful promises. Not only can you confidently take your requests to God, but you can be certain that He will hear you. And if your prayer aligns with God's will for your life, you can be certain of receiving it. But what if you're not certain your prayer is God's will? Then pray as Jesus did—"Not my will, but yours be done" (Luke 22:42).

How do these three promises from 1 John 5:14–15 affect your faith, your expectation that God will answer your prayers?

....

....

....

When you pray "not my will, but yours be done," how does that change your expectations of *how* God will answer?

....

....

....

....

....

....

....

....

....

....

....

....

WEEK 23
Faith Loves Courageously

>>>>>>><<<<<<

"Love your enemies, do good to those who hate you, bless those who curse you, pray for those who mistreat you."

Luke 6:27–28

Love . . . your enemies? Those who hate you? Who curse and mistreat you? To love like that is a risk. You could be rejected, mocked, or worse. It takes courage—the kind of courage that only comes from putting your faith in the One who unconditionally loves you. Love your enemies? Yes, that's exactly what Jesus calls you to do. Because that's the risk He took in loving you.

Loving your enemy might not change his or her heart, but it will always change yours. Do you agree with that statement? Have you seen its truth play out in your own life?

....

....

....

Is there a difficult person—even an enemy—in your life whom Jesus is calling you to love? What is one thing you can risk doing differently this week, one thing that will show that person both your love and His?

....

....

....

....

....

....

....

....

....

....

....

WEEK 24
Faith Examines Itself

〉〉〉〉〉✕〈〈〈〈〈

Be on your guard; stand firm in the faith; be courageous; be strong. Do everything in love.

1 Corinthians 16:13–14

F aith is not something you can simply check off a list. But a list—like this one from 1 Corinthians 16—*can* serve as a sort of checkup for your faith. Are you guarding your faith, continuously avoiding the sins that weaken it? Are you standing firm, relying on God's strength and not your own? Is your faith bold or weak and hidden away? Is there love in your actions and words? If your faith isn't all it should be, turn to Jesus, the One who perfects your faith.

As you consider this list, is your faith what it should be?

....

....

....

....

Faith comes from the Word of God (Romans 10:17).
Strengthen your faith by spending time in His Word.
Isaiah 40:28–31 is a great place to begin. Keep a
record here of the passages God uses to build your
faith this week.

....

....

....

....

....

....

....

....

....

....

....

WEEK 25
Faith Carries

>>>>>>><<<<<<

When Jesus saw their faith . . .

Luke 5:20

Four men carried their friend to Jesus because they believed Jesus was their friend's only hope. But the house was full and the crowds were huge, and there was no way in. Except . . . *the roof.* So up they went and down their friend went—right in front of Jesus. And a man was healed because four men were willing to carry their friend to Jesus.

Faith carries those you love to Jesus, lays them at His feet, and trusts Him to work in their lives for good. After all, He loves them even more than you do.

Those four friends refused to let a roof or a crowd come between their friend and the Savior he needed. Are you allowing anything—fear, embarrassment, awkwardness—to come between your loved one and the Savior he or she needs?

....

....

....

Who are the loved ones you most want to carry to Jesus? What steps can you take this week to lay them at His feet?

....

....

....

....

....

....

....

....

....

....

....

....

....

WEEK 26
Faith Encourages Faith

>≫≫≫≻≺≪≪≪≪

I want us to help each other with the faith we have.
Your faith will help me, and my faith will help you.

Romans 1:12 NCV

Faith is not a solitary way of life. It seeks out others of faith—to encourage and be encouraged—as you journey along together, traveling ever closer to God.

There will be days when you are the encourager, coming alongside and helping carry another's load. And there will days when you find yourself gratefully leaning on the strength of a faithful friend. Together, encourager and encouraged, you are both made all the stronger. Because faith encourages faith.

Think of the most encouraging person you have in your life. What is it about that person that encourages you? How can you cultivate that into your own life and become a better encourager too?

....

....

....

What most encourages you in your faith? Is it conversations with a faithful friend, a walk in creation, or quiet moments with the Word? Allow yourself time to be encouraged each day.

....

....

....

....

....

....

....

....

....

....

....

WEEK 27
Faith Goes and Tells

>>>>>⟩⟨⟨⟨⟨⟨

*"Go everywhere in the world, and tell
the Good News to everyone."*

Mark 16:15 NCV

G o . . . and tell." That is Jesus' command. But going and
telling takes faith. Not only faith in the One you want to tell
the world about but also faith that He will give you everything
you need to do it. When going and telling makes you want to
run and hide, remember the God who took ordinary fishermen
and transformed them into fishers of men (Matthew 4:19).

Faith doesn't hesitate to go and tell. Do you hesitate?
Why?

....

....

....

....

....

Not everyone goes and tells in the same way. It might be behind a microphone, behind a keyboard, or behind a cup of coffee shared with a friend. Write out a prayer asking God what your going and telling should look like.

....

....

....

....

....

....

....

....

....

....

....

WEEK 28
Faith Takes Risks

>>>>>>>⫘<<<<<<

"I will instruct you and teach you in the way you should go; I will counsel you with my loving eye on you."

Psalm 32:8

Faith is taking a risk. It's choosing to believe in something—in Someone—you cannot see. It's stepping out and starting the journey when you're not sure where the path will lead. It's leaving the familiar and risking the unknown. And it can be unsettling, even frightening. But it's a risk that's never taken alone. Never taken without a guide, *the* Guide, who lovingly watches over every step you take.

What risk is God asking you to take? A new venture? A new way to minister? Or simply—yet, oh so importantly—to fully put your faith in Him?

....

....

....

....

Perhaps you've already taken the risk, you've already stepped out onto the path God has put before you. What rewards are you seeing in your life? What do you need to do to ensure that you are ever tuned to His leading?

....

....

....

....

....

....

....

....

....

....

....

When Faith Is Hard

When faith is hard,
faith holds on.

Faith in Fear

＞＞＞＞＞＞＞◄◄◄◄◄◄

When I am afraid, I put my trust in you. In God, whose word I praise, in God I trust; I shall not be afraid.

Psalm 56:3–4 ESV

Fear. At times it creeps in like a shadow, chilling and cold. Other times it lunges in like a lion, seeking to shred and tear with sudden ferocity. The answer to fear is faith. But faith isn't necessarily about erasing your fears or eliminating them from your life. Instead, faith is about turning them over to the One who is bigger and stronger than all your fears. Faith trusts God to chase away the darkness, to defeat the lions, and to see you safely through to the other side.

Reading through the psalms reveals that David often dealt with fear, yet his faith in God did not waver. How do you deal with fear—the "small," daily fears and the larger, lion-sized ones? What does the way you handle your fears say about your faith?

....

....

....

What are the fears that shadow you? Are they physical or financial? Spiritual or relational? Turn to God and to His Word. What promises do you find to help you answer your fears with His faithful promises?

WEEK 30
Faith in Doubt

≫≫≫×≪≪≪

I do believe; help me overcome my unbelief!
Mark 9:24

Faith is not blind. It is with eyes wide open taking your trust and placing it in the hands of God. And it is also—with eyes wide open—taking your doubts, questions, and fears and placing them in His hands too.

Faith begs, just like that father in Mark 9, for belief to triumph over unbelief. It seeks the promised wisdom (James 1:5). And it prays for one's heart, mind, and soul to be open to the daily reminders of God's presence (Romans 1:20). Doubt doesn't make faith dead; rather, doubt should make faith busy.

What are the things and the situations that cause you to question and doubt? How might God be working in and through them?

....

....

....

....

Take a walk outside in the world God has created. Allow yourself to be swept up in the intricacies, the wonders of all He has made. What most calls your heart to believe, to have faith rather than doubts?

....

....

....

....

....

....

....

....

....

....

....

WEEK 31
Faith When You Forget

>>>>>>><<<<<<

"You of little faith. . . . Don't you remember . . . ?"

Matthew 16:8–9

More than two thousand years ago, Jesus asked His disciples the question that often plagues believers still today: "Don't you remember?"

When troubles leave you hungry for hope, when doubts threaten to capsize your trust, when waves are all you can see . . . why is it such a struggle to remember His past faithfulness? The times when hope overflowed, storms stilled, and a hand reached down to pluck you from the waves? And isn't it wonderful that God's faithfulness doesn't depend on your remembering?

In the midst of troubles and storms, do you struggle to remember all the times He has been faithful to see you through? Why do you think that happens so easily, so often?

....

....

70

Write about a time God was faithful to you. How does remembering His past faithfulness strengthen you for whatever might come your way?

....

....

....

....

....

....

....

....

....

....

....

....

....

71

WEEK 32
Faith Is Worth the Fight

>>>>>✕<<<<<

I have fought the good fight, I have finished the race, I have kept the faith.

2 Timothy 4:7

Some battles are worth the fight. The battle to keep your faith is one of them. And make no mistake, there will be days when it is a fight. When the world will challenge the very foundations of what you believe. Fight—not with fist or sword—but by burying yourself in His Presence, in His Word. Allow Him to hem you in "behind and before" (Psalm 139:5), to pick you up and carry you close to His heart (Isaiah 40:11), and to fight for you (Exodus 14:14).

Read the promises of Exodus 14:14 and Romans 8:31. Whatever the battle, when it's for your faith and for the Lord, do you ever fight alone?

....

....

....

How does faith help you fight for your faith? And, for you, why is your faith worth fighting for?

....

....

....

....

....

....

....

....

....

....

....

....

WEEK 33
Faith Runs to Jesus

>>>>>>><<<<<<

*Suddenly a furious storm came up on the lake,
so that the waves swept over the boat. But Jesus
was sleeping. The disciples went and woke him,
saying, "Lord, save us! We're going to drown!"*

Matthew 8:24–25

Yes, they were in a boat, but don't think those disciples slowly strolled over to Jesus. They scrambled, tripping over ropes and slipping across sea-drenched boards. As much as it was possible in that storm-tossed boat, they ran to Jesus.

And it will happen to you. One day, you'll see nothing but the waves, feel nothing but the fear. Run to Jesus. And you won't have to run far . . . because He's right there in the boat with you.

When Jesus woke, He asked, "Where is your faith?" (Luke 8:25). Why is it so easy for faith to falter when storms hit?

....

....

....

When you run to Jesus, He'll either stop the storm around you—or He'll stop the storm inside you. How have you seen this in your own life?

....

....

....

....

....

....

....

....

....

....

....

....

When Your Faith Isn't So Full

*When Peter saw the wind and the waves, he became
afraid and began to sink. He shouted, "Lord, save me!"
Immediately Jesus reached out his hand and caught Peter.
Jesus said, "Your faith is small. Why did you doubt?"*

Matthew 14:30–31 NCV

Sometimes you forget. Sometimes the winds and the waves
are all you can see. And for a moment, for more than a
moment, you forget *who* controls those winds and waves. But
Jesus never forgets you. He's still right there—though your eyes
are too filled with the storm to see. And when you remember,
when you call out to Him, He reaches down and plucks you from
the midst of the storm. Because God is fully faithful—even
when your faith isn't so full.

Psalm 18:16 says, "The LORD reached down from
above and took me; he pulled me from the deep
water" (NCV). Has God pulled you from the deep
waters? Even when your faith was small?

....

....

Just a few verses later in Psalm 18:19, you learn *why* God rescues you. What is that reason, and how does that bolster your faith?

....

....

....

....

....

....

....

....

....

....

....

....

WEEK 35
When God's Plans Change Everything

❯❯❯❯❯⫸❦⫷❮❮❮❮❮

Mary said, "I am the servant of the Lord.
Let this happen to me as you say!"

Luke 1:38 NCV

Mary probably planned many things for her life, but it's safe to say that Jesus wasn't one of them. Yet when the angel explained God's plan for her, she didn't falter. Her response to this path that would change her life forever was to say, "Let this happen to me as you say!" Because Mary had faith. She knew her Lord, and she knew He would walk with her every step of the way.

Has God ever asked you to walk down a life-changing path? One that completely disrupted all your plans? What was your response?

....

....

....

When you put your faith in God and His plans, what does He promise you? (Consider Proverbs 3:5–6.) Where will His paths lead you?

....

....

....

....

....

....

....

....

....

....

....

....

WEEK 36
Jesus Prays for You

"I have prayed for you . . . that your faith may not fail."
Luke 22:32

There is so much to learn about faith from Peter's mistakes. Things like, when your faith comes under attack, Jesus prays for you. When you've let Him down, He makes sure you know He still wants to see you: "Go and tell his disciples, including Peter" (Mark 16:7 NLT). And when you come back to Him, He gives you a job to do: "Feed my sheep" (John 21:17).

At one time or another, your faith will be attacked. What does Hebrews 7:25 tell you about the power of Jesus' prayers for you?

....

....

....

....

....

Do you ever relate to Peter and his struggles? Is it possible that being honest and open about your faith struggles could help someone else's faith?

....

....

....

....

....

....

....

....

....

....

....

....

WEEK 37
Faith Is Your Shield

>>>>>>><<<<<<

Take up the shield of faith, with which you can
extinguish all the flaming arrows of the evil one.
Ephesians 6:16

You are under attack, and it's likely that you feel it every day. The devil—that roaring lion, that thief, that father of lies—is always on the prowl. Not just to tempt or to trip up but to devour and destroy. But God doesn't leave you defenseless. He gives you a shield: your faith. Because when you know and believe the truths of His Word, the flaming arrows of the enemy's lies falter and fail at your feet.

What are the devil's favorite arrows to fling at your faith? Which one most often hits its mark? What are the promises from God, from His Word, that extinguish those arrows?

....

....

....

....

To whom does this battle against the devil—and it is surely a battle—belong? Consider 1 Samuel 17:47, 1 John 4:4, and 1 John 5:4. What do these verses tell you about who really fights your battle against the evil one and who wins?

WEEK 38
Imperfect Faith Is Perfected

Look only to Jesus, the One who began our faith and who makes it perfect.

Hebrews 12:2 NCV

aith begins with Jesus—believing in Him, in who He is, in what He promises. Jesus then takes those beginnings of your faith and makes them perfect, like the crayoned scribblings of a child transformed into a museum masterpiece. All the flaws and failures, all the questions and moments of doubt, are covered over with the spotless robe of His righteousness. Your faith is exchanged for His . . . and imperfection is perfected.

"While we were still sinners, Christ died for us." That's the message of Romans 5:8. What does this verse tell you about how perfect your faith has to be?

....

....

....

Abraham's faith was "credited to him as righteousness" (Romans 4:3). It was his faith that "made him right with God" (NCV). But was Abraham's faith perfect? What made his faith—in spite of its moments of imperfection—so great in God's eyes?

Faith Is for Growing

Faith is never content simply to "be." It is ever seeking to draw nearer to the heart of God.

Faith Seeks God

〉〉〉〉〉〉✕〈〈〈〈〈〈

*"You will seek me and find me when
you seek me with all your heart."*

Jeremiah 29:13

No matter where you are on your journey of faith—whether almost home, somewhere down the road, or still contemplating taking that first step to truly believe—the faithful life is a life of continual searching. Not because God hides from you. No! He *promises* to be found. But because there is always more to know about Him, always more wonders and depths to discover, always more love to embrace. Faith seeks God . . . and continually finds Him.

This process of seeking and searching is not wholly dependent upon you. In fact, Jesus said He came "to seek and to save the lost" (Luke 19:10). What does that tell you about the relationship God longs to have with you?

. . . .

. . . .

. . . .

James 4:8 offers a beautiful promise. What is that promise? How can you claim it in your life this week? Make note of all the ways God reveals Himself to you.

Your Faith Is Made More Than Enough

Jesus said, "Bring the bread and the fish to me."

Matthew 14:18 NCV

When you give your faith to Jesus—whether it's the size of a mustard seed or the size of Mars—He makes it more than enough. Like that little boy's lunch in John 6:1–13. Five little loaves and two fish transformed into more than enough to feed thousands. It's the simple act of bringing your faith to Jesus that opens up your life, your situation to the power of His touch. So that the woefully insufficient becomes more than enough. And the impossible becomes the new reality.

Is there an impossible in your life? Do the resources you have to face it seem woefully insufficient? Are you willing to entrust this impossible to Jesus?

. . . .

. . . .

. . . .

Write out a prayer here, entrusting your faith—along with your impossibles—to Jesus. Then watch and note what the power of His touch does.

....

....

....

....

....

....

....

....

....

....

....

....

Faith Is a Foundation to Build On

>>>>>⋗⋖<<<<<

Do your best to add these things to your lives: to your faith, add goodness; . . . knowledge; . . . self-control; . . . patience; . . . service for God; and . . . kindness for your brothers and sisters in Christ; and to this kindness, add love.

2 Peter 1:5–7 NCV

Your faith in God—your trust in His promises—forms the foundation for your life. But foundations are meant to be built upon. God wants you to add to your foundation goodness, knowledge, self-control, patience, service, kindness, and love. And He wants you to keep on layering them one on top of the other, until your life is a shining tower of praise pointing right to God. Salvation is your faith in the gift of God's grace (Ephesians 2:8–9). Why then is what you do—how you live—still so important?

When the world challenges you, how does faith in God help you continue to love and serve? How does Philippians 4:13 support this?

....

....

Even people who have no faith can be good, patient, and kind. But Psalm 127:1 says, "Unless the LORD builds the house, the builders labor in vain." What does that tell you about the underlying strength the foundation of faith provides?

....

....

....

....

....

....

....

....

....

....

Faith Trusts God to Finish What He Started

God began doing a good work in you, and I am sure he will continue it until it is finished when Jesus Christ comes again.

Philippians 1:6 NCV

You blew it. *Again*. The doubts. The questions. The missteps. So you beat yourself up, asking, "What kind of faith does that?" Beautiful faith. Imperfect, yes, but beautiful in the eyes of your Lord who never asked or expected your perfection. Don't give up. Carry your mistakes to the One who promises to forgive them (1 John 1:9), and allow His grace to wash you whiter than snow. Then pick up your faith, and trust Him to finish this wonderful work He has begun in you.

God will finish the work He has begun in you. That's a powerful promise. What reassurances does it bring to your journey of faith?

....

....

Have you blown it? Write out your confession—
confessing both your mistakes and your faith. Then
sit back, close your eyes, and listen as He whispers His
love and grace over you.

WEEK 43
Faith Seeks God's Guidance

≫≫≫≫✕≪≪≪≪

Show me your ways, Lord, teach me your paths.
Guide me in your truth and teach me, for you are
God my Savior, and my hope is in you all day long.

Psalm 25:4–5

Faith means not only *knowing* you don't have to do it all on your own; it also means not *trying* to do it all on your own anyway. Because you do, don't you? You have access to the One who knows all, who knows exactly the path you should take—and yet how often do you set out using only your own wisdom to guide you? Slow down, seek God, seek guidance . . . He will show you the way.

What does God promise in James 1:5? What is the only thing you have to do to access this promise? What stops you from seeking guidance?

....

....

....

Rewrite Psalm 25:4–5 in your own words, applying them to your own search for guidance in your faith.

WEEK 44
Faith Seeks God's Correction

Search me, God, and know my heart; test me and know my anxious thoughts. See if there is any offensive way in me, and lead me in the way everlasting.

Psalm 139:23–24

Living a life of faith means you want your thoughts, words, and actions to please God. You know you're not perfect, but you're trying to not be quite so *imperfect*. That's exactly the kind of humble heart God loves. When you pray to Him, asking Him to show you what needs correcting, what needs a bit more work, He will show you—and He'll guide you "in the way everlasting."

Is it easy to ask for God's correction? What makes it difficult? What makes it easier?

Write out Psalm 139:23–24 in your own words as a prayer to God. Then listen in the coming days for any corrections God reveals to you.

....

....

....

God's Word serves as a mirror, reflecting who you are and showing how much—or how little—you look like Christ. Commit to spending time in God's Word this week. Keep notes here of what it reveals to you and about you.

....

....

....

....

....

....

....

....

....

....

....

Faith Grows Deep Roots

_Just as you accepted Christ Jesus as your Lord, you
must continue to follow him. Let your roots grow
down into him, and let your lives be built on him.
Then your faith will grow strong in the truth you were
taught, and you will overflow with thankfulness._

Colossians 2:6–7 NLT

Like the seed that fell on rocky ground in Jesus' parable in
Matthew 13, faith can quickly disappear if it doesn't have
deep roots. Worries and fears, or just plain busyness and
neglect, can choke out what was once such good news. Faith—
like the seed—must be nurtured with prayer, watered with His
Word, and nourished with time spent in His presence. Then its
roots will grow deep, your faith will flourish, and your heart
with overflow with thankfulness.

Do worries and fears try to choke out your faith?
Or is it neglect and busyness that are more apt to
get in the way?

....

....

....

Think about how you can nurture your faith. Write out a plan for this week to spend time in prayer, in the Word, and in His presence.

WEEK 46
Faith Perseveres

>>>>>>>>⟩⟨⟨⟨⟨⟨⟨⟨⟨

*Consider it pure joy, my brothers and sisters, whenever
you face trials of many kinds, because you know that
the testing of your faith produces perseverance.*

James 1:2–3

onsider it pure joy . . . There are probably many things you
consider pure joy—the rainbow after the rain, a child's
laughter, a starry sky on a warm summer's night—but *trials*
aren't likely to be one of them. Yet James says it's the trials and
the testing that teach you to persevere, to weather the storms of
this life, to keep hanging on to God and His promises, and that
clinging to God . . . isn't that what gets you home to heaven?
Perhaps, then, trials really are a reason for joy.

How do trials test your faith? How do they teach
you to persevere?

....

....

....

....

Has there been a trial in your past that—while not "pure joy" at that time—tested and strengthened your faith? Can you now see the "joy" in that trial?

....

....

....

....

....

....

....

....

....

....

....

....

WEEK 47
Faith Is a Lifelong Journey

Jesus has the power of God, by which he has given us everything we need to live and to serve God. We have these things because we know him.

2 Peter 1:3 NCV

When you choose to believe the good news of Christ, you haven't "arrived at your faith destination." Faith is a lifelong journey traveled through and led by the Word and the Spirit of God. And as you journey, you carry the promise of 2 Peter 1:3 along with you: Jesus will make sure you have everything you need to serve God and live for Him. You are no destitute traveler on this journey of faith but rather a richly provisioned child of the King.

Do you remember that first step in your own faith journey? When your faith became truly your own? What do you most remember about that time?

....

....

....

Consider God's promise to you in 2 Peter 1:3. What does it mean to know that you are no destitute traveler but rather a richly provisioned child of the King?

....

....

....

....

....

....

....

....

....

....

Faith Is Rewarded

The life of faith is not an easy one,
but it is a richly rewarded one.

Faith Is Rewarded . . . with Peace

You will keep in perfect peace those whose minds
are steadfast, because they trust in you.

Isaiah 26:3

Yes, you can find peace in this world, but it is momentary and fleeting. Only faith in God can gift you with true and lasting peace (John 14:27) because God's peace isn't dependent on situation or circumstance. Instead, it is wholly dependent on trusting the One who is really in control and who loves you beyond comprehension. Thus it is yours to have in both the still, quiet times and in the windy, worrisome times.

Philippians 4:7 promises a peace that "transcends all understanding," but it is verse six that tells you how to access that peace. How is that?

....

....

....

....

When do you experience your most peaceful times? Your most turbulent times? Do they reflect the way you have—or haven't—carried your concerns to God?

Faith Is Rewarded . . . with Strength

We are pressed on every side by troubles, but we are not crushed. We are perplexed, but not driven to despair. We are hunted down, but never abandoned by God. We get knocked down, but we are not destroyed.

2 Corinthians 4:8–9 NLT

A life of faith will not be an easy life. You will be tested, challenged, even persecuted. *But . . .* you will not be crushed, abandoned, or destroyed, because the One you have chosen to put your faith in is not just a rock—He is *the* Rock (Psalm 18:2), an "ever-present help" in times of trouble (Psalm 46:1). So, yes, this world is going to throw some tough stuff at you. But hold tight to your faith . . . because your God is faithful and He is holding tight to you (John 10:28).

Isaiah 40:28–31 is a familiar passage, but take a moment to read afresh all its promises and list them out here. Which ones do you most need in your life today?

....

....

Write out a prayer here laying all your troubles and fears before God—and then praising Him for being your Rock, your Strength, your Refuge.

. . . .

. . . .

. . . .

. . . .

. . . .

. . . .

. . . .

. . . .

. . . .

. . . .

. . . .

WEEK 50
Faith Is Rewarded . . . with Comfort

Praise be to the God and Father of our Lord Jesus Christ, the Father of compassion and the God of all comfort, who comforts us in all our troubles, so that we can comfort those in any trouble with the comfort we ourselves receive from God.

2 Corinthians 1:3–4

God knows how painful this world can be. After all, He came down and got His hands dirty in the dust and sorrow of this world. Tears wet His cheeks. Pain tore at His body. Anger, betrayal, loss—He knows them all because He lived them all. One of the reasons the Son of God experienced all the ills this world has to offer was so that He could comfort you. Because there's no comfort quite so powerful as that which comes from One who has been where you are—and come through on the other side.

The Son of God left the perfection of heaven to experience all the hardships of this world . . . for you. How important are you to Him?

....

....

Psalm 23 is a beautiful illustration of the ways God walks with, comforts, and provides for His people. What are all the different ways God shows His comfort and care in this psalm? Are there other passages of Scripture you turn to for comfort?

....

....

....

....

....

....

....

....

....

....

....

WEEK 51
Faith Is Rewarded . . .
with Perspective

For our light and momentary troubles are achieving for us an eternal glory that far outweighs them all. So we fix our eyes not on what is seen, but on what is unseen, since what is seen is temporary, but what is unseen is eternal.

2 Corinthians 4:17–18

Faith will help you keep your troubles in perspective. Because while it may certainly feel as if it will go on forever—the loss, the shame, the heartache—it won't. There will be an end. You will be restored and healed and made whole again. Heaven *is* waiting for you. And whatever it is that's plaguing you today will be seen for what it truly is: a light and momentary trouble.

While 2 Corinthians 4:17 explains that your troubles are momentary, it is verse eighteen that tells you how to gain that perspective. How do you do that?

....

....

....

What is it that helps you keep troubles in perspective—a verse, a friend, quiet time with God?

Faith Is Rewarded . . . with the Spirit

"The Helper, the Holy Spirit, whom the Father will send in my name, he will teach you all things and bring to your remembrance all that I have said to you."

John 14:26 ESV

When Jesus returned to heaven, He left you with a promise: you'll never have to travel this journey of faith alone. When you put your faith in Jesus and follow Him, the very Spirit of God comes to live inside you: to whisper God's own words to your heart, reminding you of the truths you know but the world has tried to make you forget. The Spirit is always with you, to guide and to strengthen you . . . every moment of every day.

To discover more about what the Holy Spirit does for you, read John 16:13, Romans 8:26, and Romans 15:13. What do these verses tell you about the Holy Spirit and God's provision for you?

....

....

....

Because the Holy Spirit comes to live inside you, your body is transformed into the temple of God (1 Corinthians 6:19–20). Is your "temple" a place that honors God?

....

....

....

....

....

....

....

....

....

....

....